What A Piece of Work is Man

a collection of poetry

What a Piece of Work is Man
A collection of poems

By Peter Roderick Morgan © 2014

Cover and Interior Pictures by Jodi Morgan © 2013

What A Piece of Work is Man

a collection of poetry

Peter Roderick Morgan

To my Grandmother, Daisy Lilian Roderick
(1903 – 1978)

and

In memory of Paul Terry
(1956 – 1995),
who taught me the true meaning of
"Carpe Diem".

Contents

Part V

Notes

Acknowledgements

This book couldn't possibly have been written without the wonderful support and assistance of my parents, David and Heulwen Morgan, my wife, Ada, and my three lovely daughters (when they're not fighting) Jodi, Robyn and Bryony.

I would also like to record my appreciation to all the poets who have provided me with the inspiration and motivation to try my own hand at poetry. In particular, the many works of the great but anonymous Anglo-Saxon poets; Chaucer; John Donne; Milton; Tennyson; Edgar Allan Poe; and J.R.R. Tolkein, to name but a few.

I am also indebted to the many people who have provided me with the necessary muse to put pen to paper. In particular, Annie Ng, Paula Gilmartin, Helen Wood, Paul Terry and, of course, my wife, Ada.

Pete Morgan
Hong Kong
2014

Part 1

The Acropolis

As the sun shines
On the Acropolis of Athens,
The heat beats down
On the hard marble stone.
And we look at them as they stand
As many years ago.
The past comes forward
And the present goes back,
For they stand as they stood
Through years of attack.
But who are the attackers?
The wind and the rain,
Grubs and time,
Yet they stand all the same.
Can anything compare
With the temples of Athene?

Peace

And Nixon looked round,
He stood in war.
A war so bloody for its day.
He said "I'm hungry.
I'm hungry for peace".
He said "Let there be conferences"
And conferences were held.
Yet something was missing.
And then he knew.
He said "Let there be a ceasefire"
And there was a cease-fire.
But something was still wrong,
And then he knew.
He said "Let there be peace"
And peace there was.

Apocryphal Revelation

Philip and Karl went to the moon
That bright and late September noon.
Their mission was to search the ground
To see if on the surface round
The moon was made of Cheddar cheese
As had been told in histories.

      The rocket sped towards the stars;
      Their mission was not one to Mars
      But to the golden spheroid there
      Hung up at night without a care.
      At last the ship approached the moon
      And then the truth would out, and soon.

Their plane took orbit round the ground
So they had time to look around.
Karl slipped into his space suit then
And was just about to jump when
Philip said the safest thing
Would be to land and not to fling.

      Karl immediately understood.
      Philip landed as best he could
      So at last they could look around.

Karl was not sure what he had found;
A solid golden surface base
In which Philip could see his face.

"What is this strange and wondrous sight?
Surely the legends must have been right!"
Yet no Cheddar cheese could be found
No matter where they looked around.
Karl then kicked the ground in despair
And at once, a sound filled the air.

A high and vibrant cracking sound
Echoed around the luminous ground.
"Oh dear, whatever can this mean?"
No sound came, Karl could not be seen.
He had dashed to the rocket, safe,
And Philip too to there did race.

High up into the air they soared
And all this time the moon had roared.
Then all at once, she fell apart,
And what came out gave them a start.
A chicken large, three-stories tall,
Which into space began to fall.

On their return to earth again,
They tried to sleep but all in vain.
For Cheddar cheese, there was none there,

Only a chicken in its lair.
Their disappointment was so great
They decided to all relate.

At last the truth to all was known,
Despite all legends that had grown.
No cheese, Caerphilly or otherwise,
All the old legends were but lies.
So now at least it can be said,
The moon was really one big egg!

Mother's Day

I find the rhymes
Within these books
A trifle wet
In form and looks
So here I have
With due respect
Rewritten them
As you'd expect.
No soppy "Loves"
Or "Dearest Mine"
But down to earth
In word and line.
So here I write
In memory
Of all the things
You've done for me.
Now one last word
(You'll know it's true)
When I just say
A BIG THANK YOU !

In Memorium

(Dedicated to the Hapless Shakespearian Actor)

My limbs grow weary
And my tongue doth stray,
So from this place
I will away.

In minutes now
I will come back
And carry on
Where I lost track.

So wait a time
While I go find
This poxy line
Lost from my mind.

Part II

Epitaph for a Dragon

From within that dark and sterile cave
Came the smell from a dragon's grave.
The horde of silvery, shiny gold
(For any who might be so bold
To enter in that dragon's lair
And see, perhaps, how he might fare)
With dragon's bones lay strewn across the floor.

Now let us go and beat against that door
And see, with eager eyes, what lies therein;
Be it horrid crimes or callous sin.
Come adventurous and gallant stranger,
Come inside and seek the danger,
For if you don't this bitter night
Then never will you see this sight;
A sight too awful for mere mortal men.

For it is only from within a dragon's den
That the truth of war and hate
May be told, and so relate,
To those pitiful creatures once called men.
But stranger, where have you just gone?
Is this sight too horrible for you to look upon?
Dare mortal man ignore his crimes?

Instead, come down within these mines
To find a dragon long gone dead
To put the blame upon instead.

War

The crimson sky
The setting sun.
Not a time for one
To have a war.

        Then, the first shot:
        A cannon ball.
        All the men call,
        "The war's begun!"

The men mount,
The horses neigh
And the men pray
For what's to come

        The bugle calls.
        The men prepare
        While others stare
        To watch the charge.

All is over.
There were but a few
Who knew
That some would die.

The crimson sky
The setting sun.
Not a time for one
To have a war.

New Recruits

The heat beat down
and all around
sat little demons
once called men

And between these spirits
sat a god
with horns of fiery
purpled blood

And he ordered these things
(once called men)
to go and get
some more recruits

So off they went
to find some men
of evil deed

who lay in abundance
upon the earth

The Devil

And the devil came down
        to look around
for some men to fill his ranks

And the devil gave thanks
        to mortal men
who made his job easy once again.

Riddle

My lower trunk is long and stout,
A furry bush above.
My roots are sown deep down
Below the ground I love.

I need no water to survive
Nor air not sun nor rain.
But planted I just grow and grow;
And so does human pain.

And once I have been cut
And I no longer seem
To hurt and main at all:
I still can make them scream.

(What am I?)

Part III

What a piece of work is man

I

For nine months now had he grown and aged
For nine long months had his organs slaved
His pump was full and it spewed forth blood
From pulsing veins throbbed a tarnished mud
His unripe brain swam in jellied seas
A floating mass of sargasso weeds
His hands and feet were encased in slime
Like rotten twigs from primeval time
Anaemic eyes glared through bone-bleached skin
And burnt-black orbs glowered hate within
His sky was dark like some starless sleep
No light dared come in this dungeon deep
He breathed in blood and he choked on sperm
This padded cell for his life intern
This dripping mass made of drooling brain
Decided then to sow his rank grain
Which soon would grow into crooked corn
The crop of which would be dark forlorn
Then came the day for the harvest yield
To break this child from his prison sealed

21

II

The light poured in as the gates flung wide
And throbbing thighs threw the child outside
His bloody form was then hoisted high
Like some trophy 'gainst a blood-shot sky
The weak frail form felt his skin cut deep
And some dangling thread piled in a heap
His velvet coat was ripped from his back
And thrown away like some peasant's sack
His naked form was then battered well
Until a scream from his lips should swell
These last few months would remembered be
The blood the pain and the misery
His path was set and he knew his role
The death of men would be now his goal
The pain he felt would be felt by them
No one exempt he would all condemn
And like his coat he would rip their clothes
And like his back he would beat their backs
And like his skin he would cut their skins
And like his scream he would make them scream

And such has it been through all history
For the seeds of death lie in infancy.

Rebirth (of a world gone mad)

I

'Tis only now that the earth doth die
that the people come out, to weep, to cry.
And when the doves fly o'er the land,
the people cry for nought doth stand.
And the bells from hell do loudly knell;
they of the end of the world do tell.
But not yet one has ears to hear;
their minds were filled with awesome fear.
And when the plagues from the sky did fall,
the people crumbled, not one, but all.
No choosing now, this hideous day,
all fall prey to death's dark sway.

II

Darkness. The earth lies alone and dead.
But in that death a Child was born
Who remembers the ways forlorn.
The gods had not this battle won
for with the sinking of the sun
The Child arose and shook his fist
and the bloated sun glowed fiery red
And shone about his milk-white head.
The blood of ages past did show
and deep within the Child would grow.
The gods turned round and walked away
and waited for their reckoning day.

The Dogs

In the water-crowned cobbled corners,
The bins lay on their side,
And there, besides an upturned cart,
Sat dogs with bloodstained hides.

They ate the rubbish from the street
As neon lights shone down.
They saw the pimps and prostitutes
Head for the noise filled town.

From time to time a car shot by
And dazzled them with fear;
The blinding light bit deep, so deep,
They forced an outlaw tear.

Then once again the clouds came back
And brought with them a rain
That fell and splattered on the stones
And left a ripe-red stain.

The gravel grooves grew in the dust
While men sped home to wives.

The dogs sat silent in the rain;
In ones and twos and fives.

The street lay silent in the mist
As shadows fluttered past.
The only sound was padded feet
That sped to end their fast.

Once again (in twos and threes)
The dogs just sat and stared.
Their eyes lay wide and blood-shot red
And milk-white teeth lay bared.

And then a sound streaked through the night
Of heavy shoes on stone.
Ears pricked up and the breaths came hard:
A rough clad man.... alone!

II

The man was singing hard that night
As cheer against the rain;
A piercing, biting, tearing wind
Blew Up and down again.

His coat flew back, a comet's tail,
That flushed and flailed around.

He tried and tried to keep it down
To stop that soaring sound.

It was the wind and the rustling trees
That hid the shuffling paws.
The man stared hard into the night
And saw their gaping jaws.

The dogs moved fast in front of him
And blocked the path ahead.
The man stared through dilated eyes
At dogs with teeth stained red.

He focused hard upon the dogs
Through slowly swimming eyes.
The beer swished round inside of him
And said he saw but lies.

he thought he saw but images
From story tellers books;
But what he saw before his eyes
Were dogs with evil looks.

he looked at them, and they at he,
But neither gave their ground.
The man stood grinning at the sight;
The dogs, they made no sound.

A step was taken by the man
Amongst the heaving limbs.
This living fence was far too strong
For now these were not games.

III

The man reeled back, fear in his eyes,
The dogs they howled a dirge,
They sang a symphony of death
To kill this frightened scourge.

The man fell down beneath their weight;
Their hairy throbbing skin
Tearing against his milk-white flesh,
Their mouths like Pierrot's grins.

And then it came, a surge of pain,
That made a scream shoot out
And sent his body writhing hard
As jaws locked on his throat.

His eyes looked up in fear and pain
And saw their snarling teeth.
His flesh gave way before their jaws
And rubbish formed his wreath.

For all this time the wind had roared
And rain had splattered hard.
The trees had rustled in the wind;
Below, the noise filled town.

So is it any wonder then,
That his screams had died away
Without a moments pause, while he
Had on the pavement lay.

The day would come when all would know
Of this night's sordid deed:
"A man was murdered by a gang",
That's how the papers read.

The dogs moved off, their stomachs full.
The man lay torn and gashed.
For now the dogs had come a struck
And nor were they the last.

Nemesis

Out of the misty, mirey moor,
Silently strode the Sentinel.
Thought to slay those heinous men
Who killed his cubs on a cold, cold night.
Caught in a cadence of captured dreams
His anger grew, his hatred swelled
As he ploughed painfully past
The windswept world. The wish
To burst those brazen, birnied bodies
Loomed large in lamentatious thoughts
As his sad, sorrowful steps sought
The mind-path of the mirthless road;
Drove deeper into hidden, hallucinatory memories.

Mingled with mind-maddening myths
Of Adam and his abject spouse
He thought, how through their deed
God gave grievous, gasping torment
To the siblings of silent sin
And cast them, cut them down
To depths of dire, dismal doom.
Nor was the plague of painful poison
Sucked and spat out with speedy haste
For God's foe from forlorn days

Made manifest his monstrous mind
And tossed through turbulent treadways
Those hapless, hell spawned hosts
To swim by sodden senseless shores
And creep by caustic, quagmired coasts.
All these and other heartfelt thoughts
Grew and groaned in his gangerous mind
Till his torment troubled tale
Tore into his tortillious limbs
And screams of sudden spite
Pulsed, pounding in his perilous veins.

Mankind murmured and moaned
In their frightened, fearful folly
At the shrill and septic sodden sound.
The hoary hairs on hero's heads
Stood up and trickled sweaty blood.
The guilt of gain grasped tightly round
And offerings and oratories flowed.
But what are baleful beads and
Trinket coloured toys to they
Who suffered soundly, sadly
Because of Adam's single sin.
The apples laid on ardent alters
And jewels, gems like jaded stars
Were smashed into a thousand suns.
The gifts to gods, grown from guilt,
Were torn and tempered tame.

The last stronghold of screaming man
Had been burst and broken forth
And now, for all those eons past,
The sentinel, the nemesis,
The guardian of a world gone mad
Strode fast, and stripped of flesh
Those men who in distant memories
And mirth filled songs had claimed
Were champions, the sons of God himself.

The blood burst forth from broken wounds
And eyes were knocked in gnarled and knotted flesh
And teeth ploughed into pox-scarred skin.
Upon this battle-field of blood
The cadavers cried in broken song.
They lowed a lamentatious lay
And those heroes, once called men,
Were by devils damned to hell
So that at last but one remained,
Himself a child, a spawn of hell,
A Sentinel, A nemesis,
The guardian of a world gone mad.

The Oak

The dark oak
A knotted tree
    Timbrous
In the dark
Of man's bleak mind

        At the edge
        Of sanity
            Gangerous
        Rotted wood;
        Velvet Lichen

Serpent leaves
Smothering all
    Suffuse
Verdant grass;
Emerald rot

        Maggots nest
        Crawling larvae
            Gestate
        hatch through skin;
        Gnarled eruption

Screams of pain
Through snarling bark
 Porous
Blood of sweat;
Festering sores

   Darkening wood
   Nefarious black
    Sombrous
   Darkening road;
   Vapid velvet

At the edge
Of consciousness
 Timbrous
Wood demons
Eat man's bleak soul

   The dark oak
   A rotted skin
    Madness
   Screams in earth:
   Its living grave.

Part IV

The Quest

    We came to a wall
And such a wall it was;
Cascading lichen
Suffused the cracks and joints
And the giant's work
Creaked and groaned with age.

    We came to a hill
Where legends dwelt in war;
Where heroes lay
And battles stormed and raged,
Where bodies paled
And bleached beneath the sun.

    We came to a town
And we fell among the thieves;
They robbed us bare
And they stole our wealth.
We came away
No richer than when born.

    We came to a tree;
A gallows post it made.
A corpse was swinging high

And jet-black ravens cawed aloud
And left his eyes
Pleading, bleeding hollow holes.

    We came to a sea
And stood on billowed shores.
The sea kings laughed
And tossed on snow-capped waves.
The sea was cold
And salt scratched open wounds.

    We came to a door
And such a door it was;
Sad and somber black,
Huge timbers felled in nordic woods
Where midnight suns
Beckon home the lost.

    We came to a throne
That glistened with jeweled studs;
Its brilliant light
Sent shivered pain and cut-glass shards
Into our questing eyes.
The blood fell thick
Upon our naked, stainéd souls.

    We came to a man
And such a man was he;

A lord, our lord,
A man unlike all other men.
But blind we came
And we saw no one there.

    We came to a room,
A floodlit, crowded room.
We cried, we screamed;
The blood was still crust hard on us.
The journey was to start again
To see the pain god gave to men.

Death in Venice

The golden palistrade is shining in the night,
The rats are running circles and they're hiding in their fright.
The moon is full and the stars are bright,
yet somehow, the scene, it doesn't seem right.

> There's something in the wind
> There's something in the air
> The gondolas are sinking
> The old men sit and stare.

Sitting on the beach is a single lonely chair;
Swinging on a post is a boy with lovely hair.
The waves are pounding up against the chair
And the boy on the lamppost doesn't even care.

> There's something by the sea
> There's something on the beach
> The painted walls are peeling
> The seagulls scream and screech.

The painted parasols are rustling in the wind;
The flies are stalking steadily a man who thinks he's sinned.
The thick black dye is trickling down his sweaty neck;

The beach-hut house is tumbling, a tussled, tumbled
wreck.

There's something in his eyes
There's something in his breath
The beach is now a graveyard
The deck chair is a headstone.

The hotel lobby's empty, the flowers have all withered,
The flagstones have all cracked, the grass is growing
through them.
The chairs have toppled over, there's no one left to right
them;
There are no sounds of footsteps on the hardened marble
floor.

There's something in the breeze
A ruby-red lipped kiss
From a boy with lovely hair.
There's been a death in Venice.

Death in a chair
On the beach
To the screech
Of a gull
Here in Venice.

Amore del Porcile

The poets write of love and life,
Of struggle and eternal strife.
They try to rhyme and harmonise;
Turn blood to wine and truth to lies.

There is more flesh and raging blood
(Than in a poet's murky mud)
In one small kiss, or one cold squeeze,
Or tingly, tickly, taunting tease.

Where are these things in poet's rhymes?
They talk of love and rosy times;
Of pearl-white teeth and ruby lips;
Of raven hair and sultry lips.

But what of moans and passions spent?
And what of limbs and torso bent?
Of sucking mouths and scorching lips;
Throbbing gasps as in he slips?

O poets, have you ever loved
Beyond your aery, milk-white doves?
Where is the tangy scent of lust;
The acrid smell of passions musk?

42

There is no art in rhyming lines!
To wallow, as if mud-caked swines
In lustful passions primal glee;
Now that, to me, is poetry!

Beatae Memorie

O face too perfect,
O body divine.
You sublime creation
Who'll never be mine.

Living in memories,
Translucent reflections;
How will I live
Without your attentions.

Already I wane
In dark, distant dreams.
Without you I die;
My sighs turn to screams.

O let me adore you,
Blissful, benumbing,
My opium of joy.
Peace, only death may bring.

Crusty, Grizzled Gripers

crusty, grizzled gripers that we are,
we said no way, no how, no chance
to love and life and nature's way.

my tangled, tussled tepid bed
will shake and squeak to no-one's play
but ride and rock to my own tune.

the sizzling, sozzling scent of eggs
and bacons turning, burning in the pan
will not be heard nor borne nor felt.

the soggy, sodden sweating pores
of laden-lust on kitchen floors
are sickly sores of sordid lust.

the shadowed bags of sleepless nights
and dripping sacks of dung-filled pants
are parent's sorrows not mine to share.

but caustic, cynic tyrants, we, we fell
and fired from greater heights and saw a life
we thought we saw and saw, we thought.

a love, a life, a line, allay all fears
that you see and see again with open eyes
what yet there is and can be yet.

when cankered, wrinkled, wretched men
fall into lust and love and life
there is a sudden surge of sorrow

that hours, seconds, days and months
gave way to nothing, nothing spent
when love and life are heaven's gift

that spans the eons, centuries old,
and runs a turning spiral wheel
to heaven and, in the end, to you.

If.....

if i could sing or shout or jump
and touch the moon with joy
then i would dance and sing out loud
that i'm in love with you

if i could count the stars above
or pick up all the grains of sand
then i would keep them in a treasure box
to show my love for you

if i could run a hundred miles
and swim the oceans large
then i would scale the highest mounts
and do it all for you

if every poem was meant for you
and every book your heart
then i would read them all again
to share my love for you

if every night was like your hair
and every dawn your eyes
then i would watch the skies all day
to see what love can be

if i could travel far and wide
and see a thousand lands
there still would only be one sight
and that would be of you

if i could journey to the stars
where galaxies revolve
the brightest flame up in the sky
would be the light from you

if my days were running short
and winter coming fast
then i would think of seasons past
when i spent spring with you

but last of all and most of all
if i could say forever more
that i love you and love you true
then that at last is love.

Ode to St. Valentine

From deep dark mists
That swirled in ages past,
There have been men
And prairies vast.

    The men, they hunt
    And fires keep,
    While women sang
    And babies sleep.

They lived a life
From day-to-day,
No time for rest
Or children's play.

    As deep dark mists
    Fled with the light
    The hunt had stopped
    With wars to fight.

The women sat
And waved farewell
As valiant men
Climbed hill and dell.

They fought on hills
And died on dales
While women sang
And wept in bales.

And as the mists
Fled far from sight
A time had passed
Of wrong to right.

The men stayed home,
The wars long gone,
While women played
And sang their song.

I thank the lord
The mists have gone
And you are here
To sing your song.

The wars are past,
And here I rest
Alone with you;
Forever blest.

Part V

For Paul

There was a time, when we were young,
That we could climb, and we would run,
    Up Morgan Trails
    Rougher than Wales
Through Sai Kung hills and Lantau dales.

There was a time, when we were young,
That we would bask under the sun,
    From Repulse Bay,
    To Mandalay,
From dawn of morn to dusk of day.

There was a time, when we were young,
That we would sail or seek some fun,
    From Disco Bay,
    To Santa Fé,
At speeds and knots that would dismay.

There was a time, when we were young,
On motorbikes down roads we'd gun,
    From Tai Mei Tuk
    To any nook,
Our engines roared and metal shook.

There was a time, when we were young,
We thought the world was ours to run,
    To change the tide,
    To walk with pride,
To run this life like a coaster-ride.

There was a time, when we were old,
When seconds ticked and minutes rolled,
    And we could see
    How it would be
And felt our own mortality.

There was a time, when we grew old,
That we could see the young as bold,
    Who failed to see
    (As you and me)
Our weakness and our frailty.

There is a time, as now we stand,
To face the world, both hand in hand,
    To lead us through
    This human zoo
Where you are me, and I am you.

There is a time, as all else fades
To see the world without our shades;
    To see the blues
    And glorious hues.

To win this fight; not dare to lose.

This is a time to fight, to win,
A time to start and to begin.
 To find our place
 In this proud race
Let's run together, pace for pace.

untitled

I

    i am afraid
and fear befriends me
    i go alone
and the shadows enclose me
    one last sigh
and the clouds bring their rain
    one final sleep
and the earth enfolds me
    one last goodbye
and my friends all surround me
    one final song
and the snows hum around me
    this is the end
and all those that knew me
    speak their farewells
and my friends all then leave me

II

    they in their sighs
see no cleansing rains wash me
    they in their sleep
see no welcoming earth
    they go alone
but the world embraces me
    they are afraid
but no fear holds me
    my final hymn
is sung loud and with joy
    my fear is crushed
and my dreams fall like snow
    the earth is my mother
and i go not alone

The Phoenix

it seems
as though the world
were washed way

as if
the circling stars
had stopped their play

it seems
as though the sea
died on the sand

as if
a smothering mist
hid an ancient land

it seems
as though the oaks
crashed to the ground

as if
the whistling wind

had stopped its sound

it seems
as though the snows
melted in death

as if
the voice of god
had lost its breath

it seems
as though my life
had died today

as if
within a grave
my body lay

it seems
as though the earth
gave way for me

as if
to show me now
its mystery

II

it seems
as though a fire
bit through my veins

as if
a wind blew through
my lung-racked pains

it seems
as though the dark
fled from my light

as if
a thousand stars
shielded their sight

it seems
as though the sky
flared with my heat

as if
the surging fire
made seas retreat

it seems
as though i flew

a phoenix rare

as if
the sky were mine
ethereal aire

it seemed
as though the world
were washed away

but now
a blood-shot sky
sped new-borne day

The beginning

Notes to the Poems

In Alphabetical Order

The Acropolis (Athens, 1972): I was visiting Athens on a school cruise when I wrote this poem. The ship's captain was running a poetry competition and a poem about the Acropolis seemed a suitable and perfect subject for my entry. The good news was that I actually won second prize for my age group. The bad news was that the prize was a book about poetry which, at the time, hardly enthralled me. I did keep that book for quite a few years and it did prove useful for some of my later poetic efforts. If I'd known what the prize was going to be, though, I probably wouldn't have bothered entering the competition in the first place.

Amore del Porcile (Sydney, Australia, 1985): This poem is one of only two poems written on request (the other is *For Paul*, which can also be found in this collection). At the time, I was staying for a few days with a friend in Sydney while traveling through Asia and the South Pacific and she asked me to write a poem for her before I flew off to Fiji. The subject matter pretty much presented itself from real life and the decision to subvert the poetic love-poem genre worked nicely for the more earthy content of the poem,

Apocryphal Revelation (UK, 1976): I wrote this poem for another competition; this time for Golden Lay Eggs™ which pretty much dictated that the subject matter had to be about eggs. I thought that playing on an old myth, that the moon is made of cheese, and exchanging it for a new myth would be quite fun. I again won second prize and a month's supply of Golden Lay Eggs (I think I preferred the poetry book!).

Beatae Memorie (UK, 1978): Whilst in my final year at University, I went to visit a friend who was studying at Manchester University. We went to a rock concert and there, right in front of me, was the most beautiful girl I had ever seen. After we left the concert, I was ridden with regret that I would never see her again or have a chance to speak with her. I consoled myself with the poem.

Crusty, Grizzled Gripers (Hong Kong, 1988): John Donne was a big influence on me poetically, particularly his ability to produce complicated themes with wonderfully convoluted language. My intention was to do something similar with this poem, albeit not quite as successfully.

The Devil (UK, 1975): Continuing the theme started in *New Recruits*, this poem reiterates the fact that if you needed to find suitable candidates for hell, you need look no further than around you.

Death in Venice (Hong Kong, 1982): I remember watching Visconti's movie "Death in Venice" and thinking that whilst the images in the film were very powerful, the film as a whole was pretty boring so I decided to edit the film down to a more manageable and evocative length.

The Dogs (UK, 1978): I had a thing for Hammer Horror films when I was younger and thought that it was perhaps about time that someone started writing cinematic-like horror poems.

Epitaph for a Dragon (UK, 1975): I had just read C. S Lewis's "Voyage of the Dawn Treader" and I was intrigued by the notion that dragons might once have been humans and how they might be blamed for the woes that humans inevitably face.

For Paul (Hong Kong, 1995): This poem was written on the request of my very close friend and orienteering partner, Paul Terry, who at the time was dying of cancer Paul very much epitomized the happy-go-lucky bon vivant and lived his life to the fullest. I read this very personal poem to him shortly before he died and his appreciation is all the recognition a writer could ever want. This book is dedicated to Paul.

In Memorium (UK, 1978): I was acting in quite a lot of plays during my 6th Form years and always worried that, one-day, I'd forget my words. As most of the plays were by Shakespeare, I thought it would be useful if I had a quick poem, in the style-of, that I could quickly fall back on if I ever did forget my words. The theory was that I'd just recite this poem, walk off the stage, check my lines and return, hopefully with no one the wiser. I never did forget my words so I never got to see if it would have worked.

Mother's Day (Hong Kong, 1988): I had a tendency to write poems for special occasions as a way of producing something very personal for the recipient. As many of those poems were very person specific, they haven't been included in this collection. I have included this one though, as it is very much about the universal theme of appreciation for your mother whilst, again, trying to subvert the poetic genre by attempting to be both self-knowing and critical of poetic conventions.

Nemesis (UK, 1980): During my first year at University, we studied a lot of Anglo-Saxon poetry, especially Beowulf. Although I hated all the translating we had to do, I really enjoyed the alliteration and imagery that the poems conjured up. I also read John Gardner's "Grendel" that retold the story from the monster's perspective and I decided to redo the poem from Grendel's perspective and to show how, perhaps, he was the victim rather than the Danes.

New Recruits (UK, 1975): The idea that Hell needed refilling was an intriguing one and, where else to get more recruits, than on earth, where war, pestilence and deprivation seem to be so rampant.

The Oak (UK, 1980): This was conceived as an aural tone poem in which the words were supposed to create the creaking sounds of the oak trapped in the ground.

Ode to Saint Valentine (Hong Kong, 1990): Written as a paean to celebrate the incessant efforts, throughout time, to find love.

Peace (UK, 1971): This poem was written after watching Richard Nixon announce on TV a cessation of hostilities, bringing about the end of the Vietnam War. It seemed to be such a momentous occasion, after such a long and grueling war, that I was reminded of the opening lines of Genesis, when God brings light out of darkness.

The Phoenix (UK, 1981): I wrote this poem immediately before leaving the UK for Hong Kong to take up employment with the Royal Hong Kong Police. It was also written as a farewell present to my, then, girlfriend. Leaving for Hong Kong very much felt like leaving my past behind and starting something new and the idea of a phoenix very much sprang to mind.

The Quest (Hong Kong, 1982): I was always intrigued with the concept of questing but always wondered what would happen if you actually came across what you were seeking without properly recognising it or if you didn't actually like what you found.

Rebirth (of a World Gone Mad) (UK, 1977): I went through a bit of an apocryphal phase during my teenage years and was concerned that mankind was very much bringing about its own demise and that the gods, whoever they might be, might actually welcome this.

Riddle (UK, 1980): I was greatly influenced by the Anglo-Saxon poets and although it's mostly the epics that are remembered (*Beowulf*, *The Battle of Maldon*, etc), the Anglo-Saxon riddles were almost haiku-like in their simplicity and structure. The answer to this particular riddle? An atomic explosion.

Untitled (UK, 1980): Was written on the death of my maternal grandmother, Daisy Lillian Roderick (1903 - 1980), at 9am, 4 November 1980. She was a strong believer in God and a regular churchgoer but, just before she died, she admitted to being afraid, despite her unyielding belief in an afterlife. Even though I was not, myself, a believer, this doubt affected me deeply until I realized that, whatever your belief system, there really was no need to be afraid as, eventually, we all go back to the welcoming embrace of the earth.

War (UK, 1975): I remember watching the movie "The Charge of the Light Brigade" and thinking that, despite the impressive arrays of uniforms and apparent glamour o war, the inevitable truth is that war can only lead to destruction and deprivation on a massive scale Unfortunately, this reality is often forgotten, especially b our politicians who initiate the hostilities in the first place.

What a Piece of Work is Man (UK, 1978): I was studying for my A-levels and also preparing for the S-leve English exam when my English teacher mentioned tha there was also a Creative Writing exam that we could try The choice was either a 2,000 word essay or a poem so went for the easier of the two options. I forget where the idea originally came from but it certainly got people talking after they read the poem (and some even worried abou my mental health given the rather vivid Hieronymus Bosch-like imagery). The poem itself was written more a an intellectual and poetic exercise so there wasn't really much for them to worry about. I was pleased to see, much later, that an article suggested that mental problems may indeed start as early as in the womb, which nicely added credence to my thesis that the trauma of child-birth car really mess you up (and Larkin thought it was your parents!). I even managed to pass the Creative Writing exam.

Index of Titles

Index of First Lines